Sing in a Season

for SATB and piano or small ensemble

vocal score

OXFORD
UNIVERSITY PRESS

OXFORD
UNIVERSITY PRESS

Great Clarendon Street, Oxford OX2 6DP,
United Kingdom

Oxford University Press is a department of the University of Oxford.
It furthers the University's objective of excellence in research, scholarship,
and education by publishing worldwide. Oxford is a registered trade mark of
Oxford University Press in the UK and in certain other countries

ISBN 978-0-19-356304-9

Music and text origination by Katie Johnston
Printed in Great Britain on acid-free paper by
Halstan & Co. Ltd, Amersham, Bucks.

Contents

Composer's note

Sing in a Season was written for the 50th anniversary of the Plano Civic Chorus, which began in the autumn of 2022. The request for this piece came from their conductor, Ralph Stannard, in early 2021, when we were slowly beginning to emerge from the Covid pandemic. Under the circumstances, we felt we needed a piece that could express what music, and particularly singing, which we had all missed so much, might mean to us. The poet Charles Bennett, in his three elegant and ultimately transformative poems, urges us to look to the diversity and richness of the surrounding natural world for ways to find our voice. The work concludes with an inspirational call from Charles's pen with the words: 'So may our lives, improvised as we go along, now and then take flight to become a song'.

Duration: *c.*15 minutes

An alternative accompaniment for small ensemble (fl, ob, cl in A, hn in F, timp, org) is available for purchase (ISBN 978-0-19-356581-4)

Commissioned for the 50th anniversary of the Plano Civic Chorus; Ralph F. Stannard, Artistic Director

Sing in a Season

1. Follow the music

Charles Bennett (b. 1954)

BOB CHILCOTT

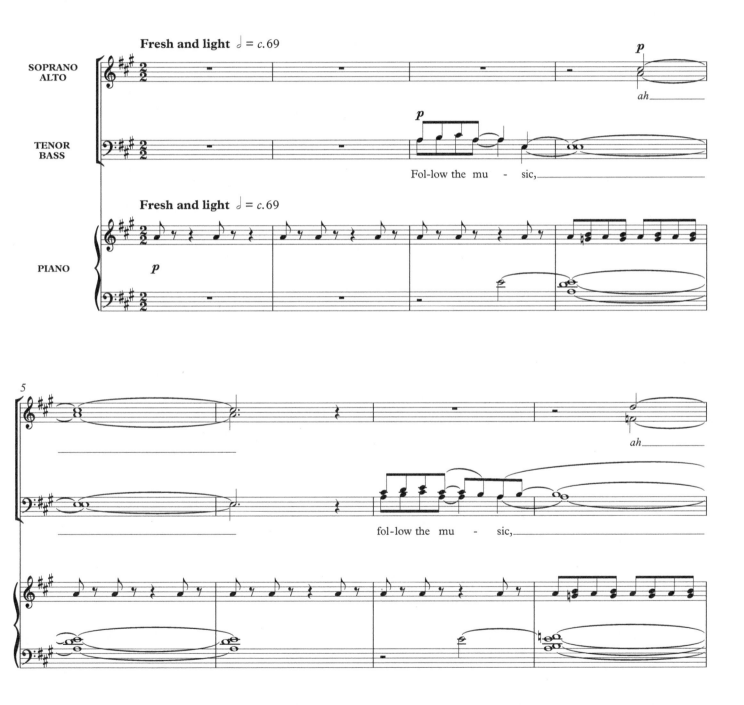

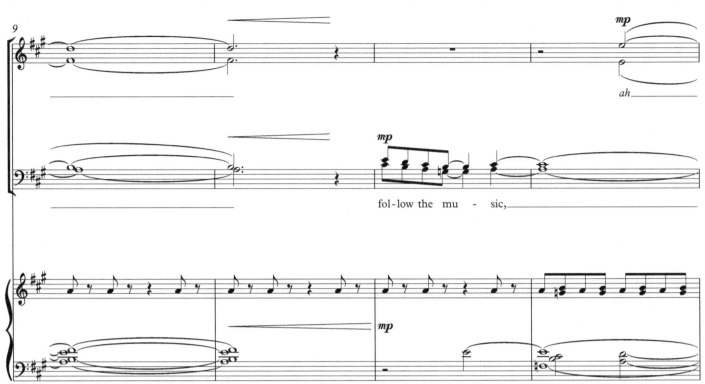

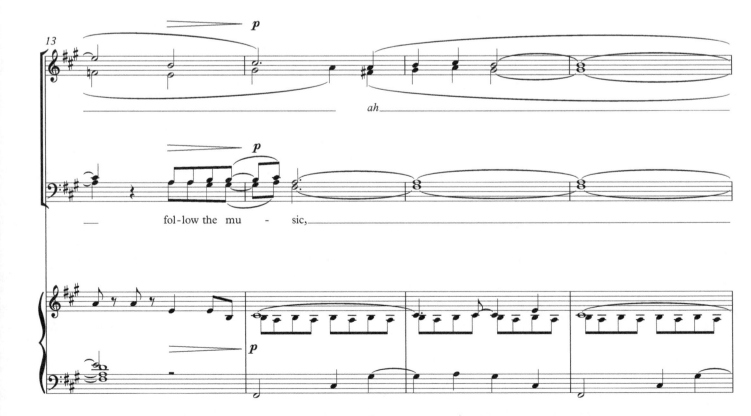

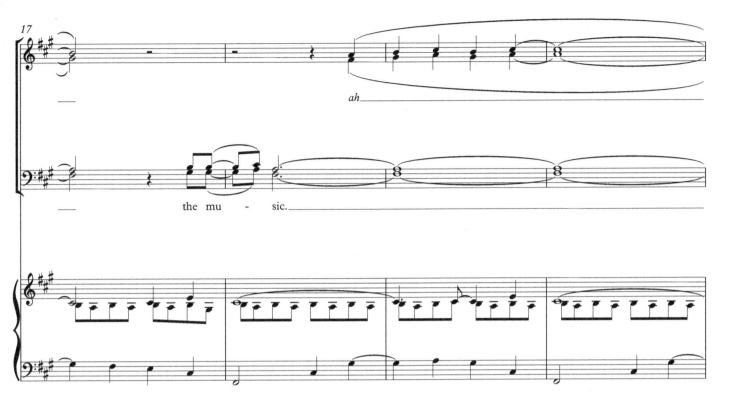

ah_____

the mu - sic._____

I   move,____   I____ move through the wood   on tip - toe_____

on

from one song, from one song to the next._____

tip - toe, tip - toe, to_____ the

bright_____ trail, a bright_____

Their mu - sic is a bright_____ trail, bright_____

next._____

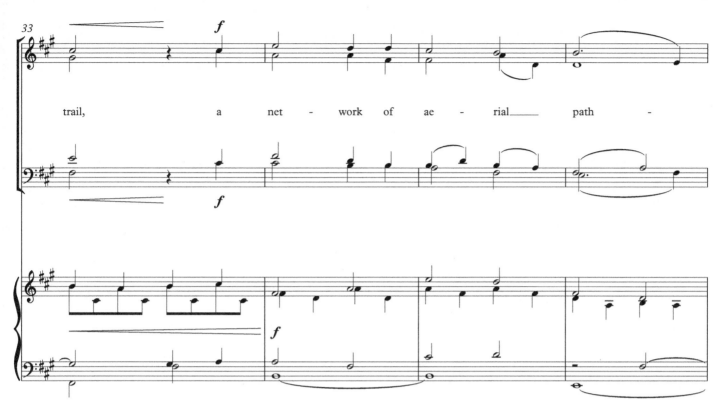

trail,   a   net - work of   ae -   rial_____ path -

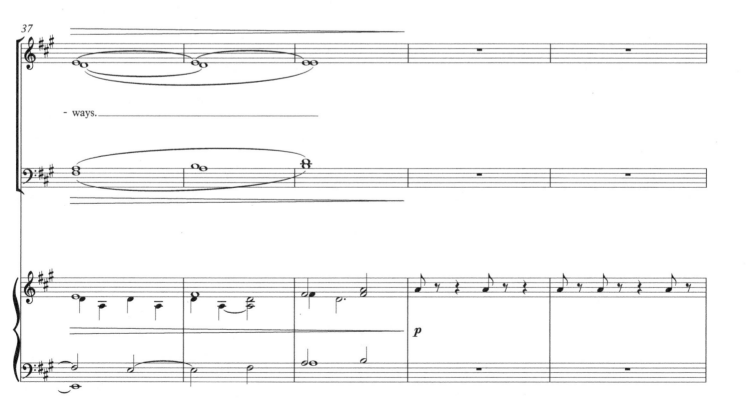

- ways._____

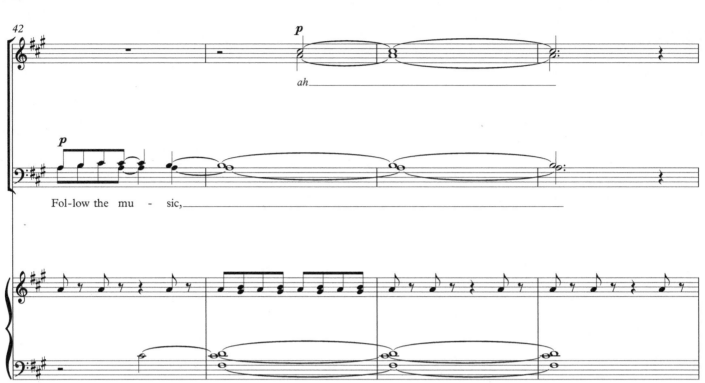

ah_____

Fol-low the mu - sic,_____

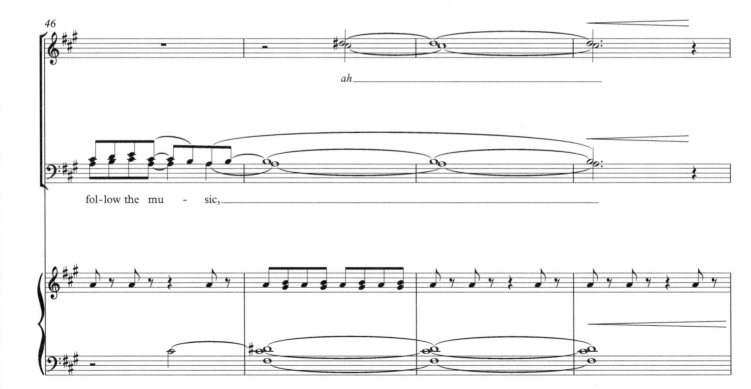

ah_____

fol-low the mu - sic,_____

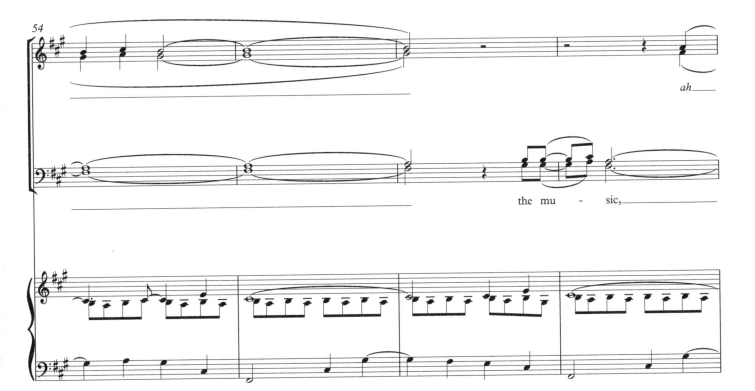

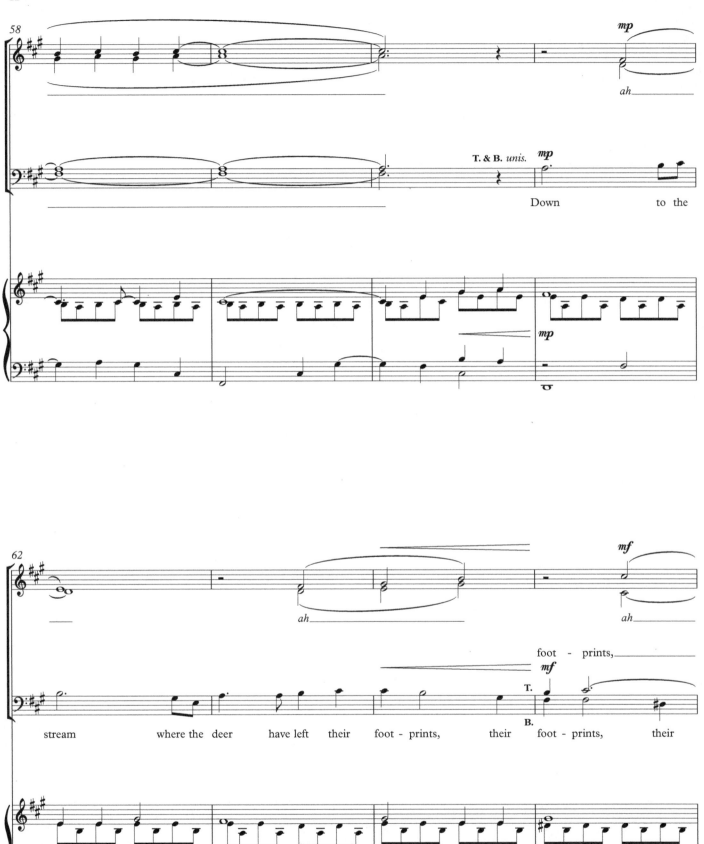

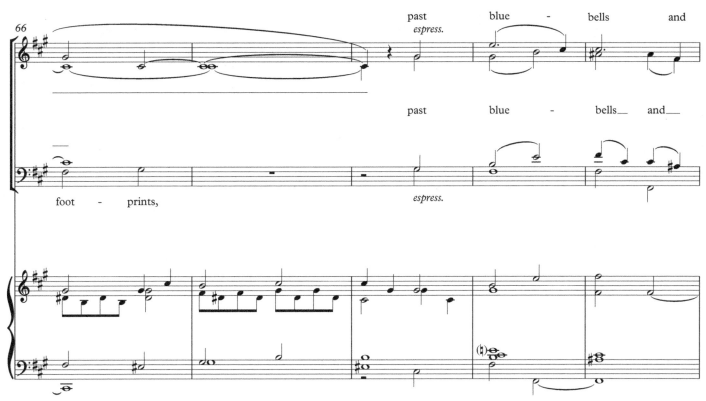

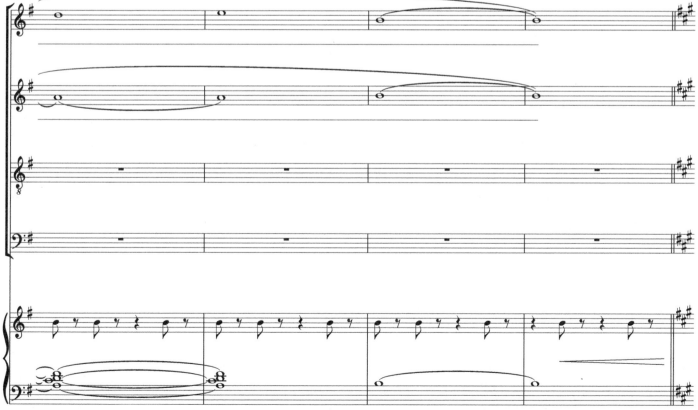

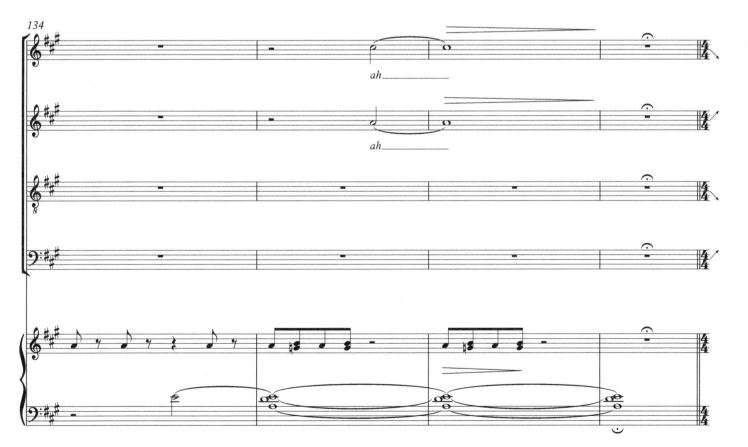

2. A Gift so in Tune

A de-so-late__ beach   As day de -

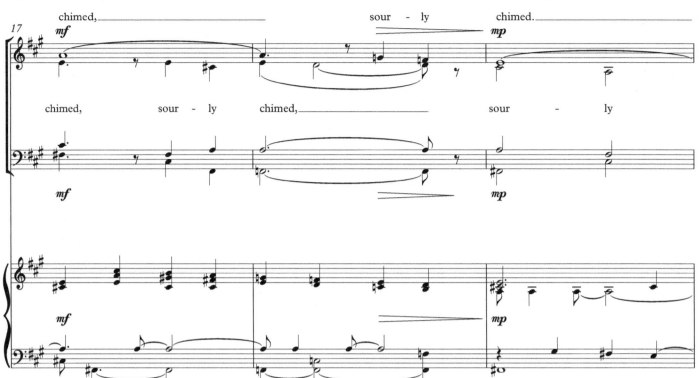

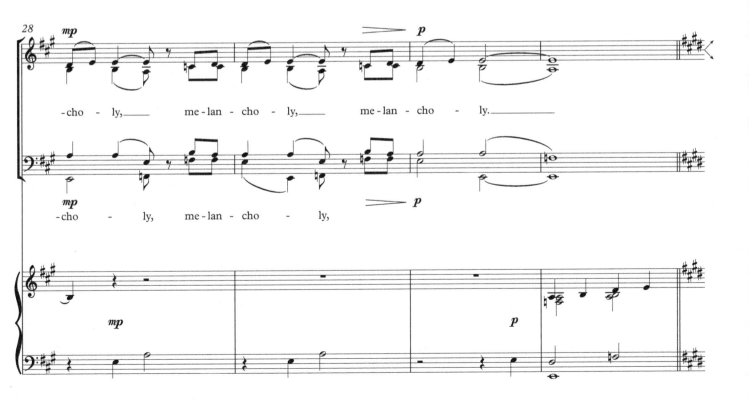

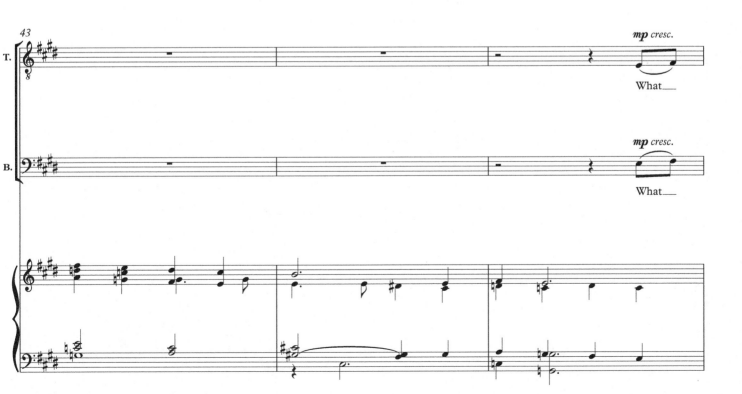

poco rit.

a tempo

Some_ sor - row, yes,_____

Some sor - row, yes, some sor - row,___

Some sor - row, yes, some sor - row,

Some sor - row, yes, some sor - row,___

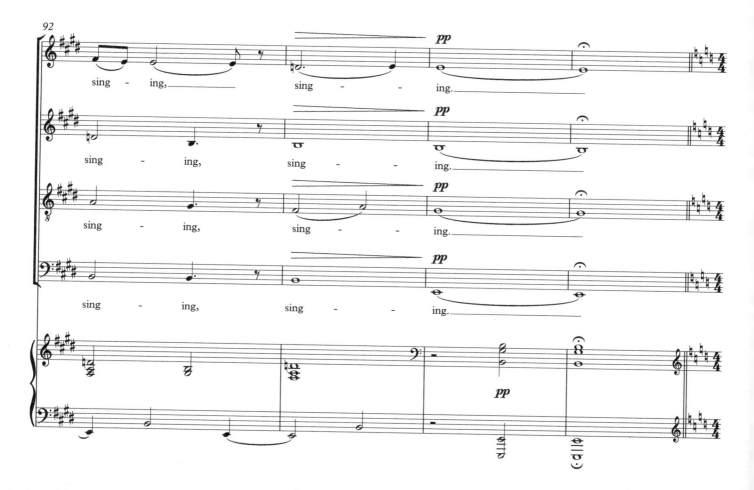

3. Sing in a Season

danced,_____ danced, on___ the wind,_ the wind,_____

laughed and danced___ on___ the wind,_____ on___ the wind,_____

and the shape they cre-

38

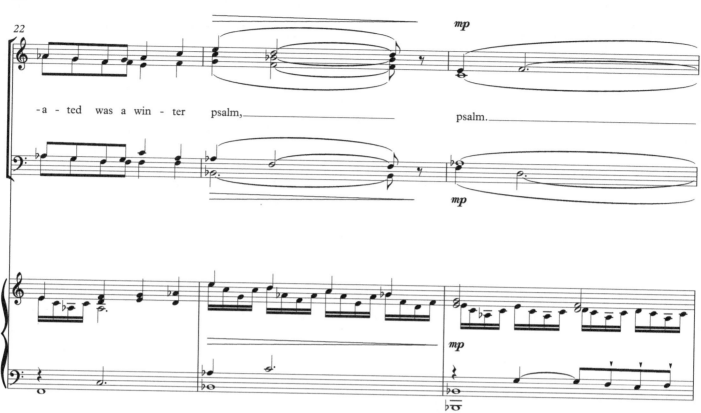

-a - ted was a win - ter psalm, psalm.

And then I knew, and

made, from those dark, dark_____ notes,_____ dis -

and made,_____ made_____ from those dark notes,

-joint - ed har - - mo - ny,

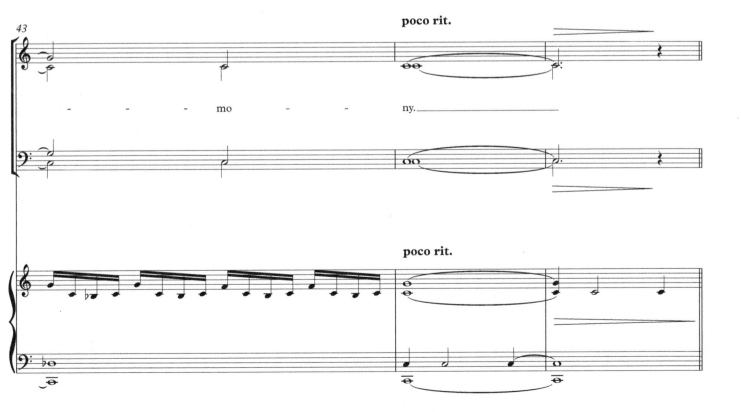

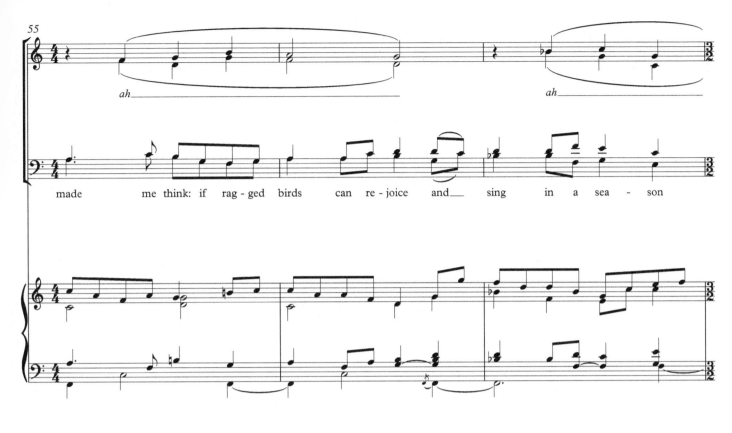

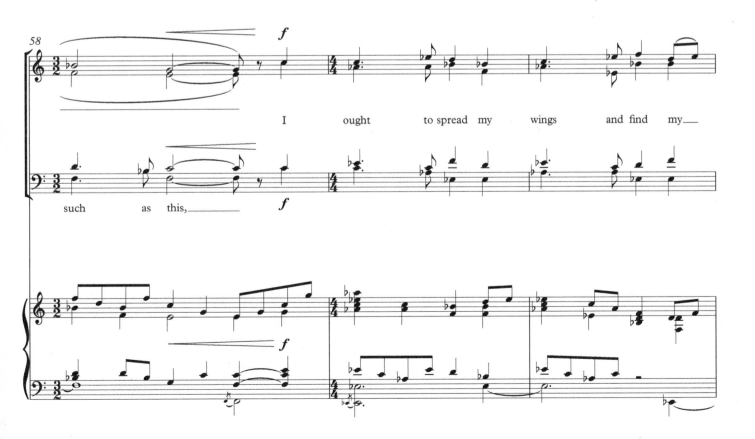

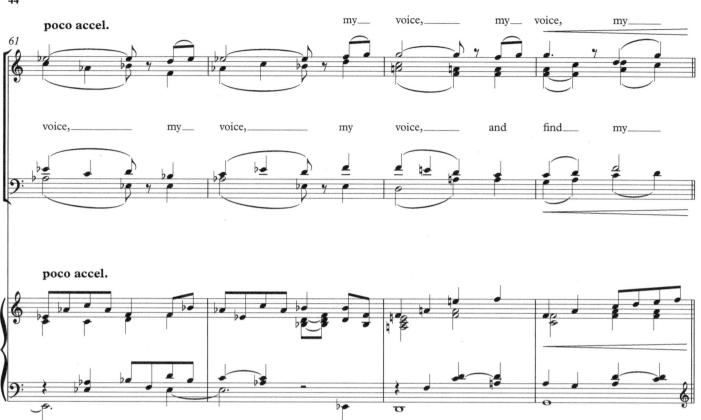

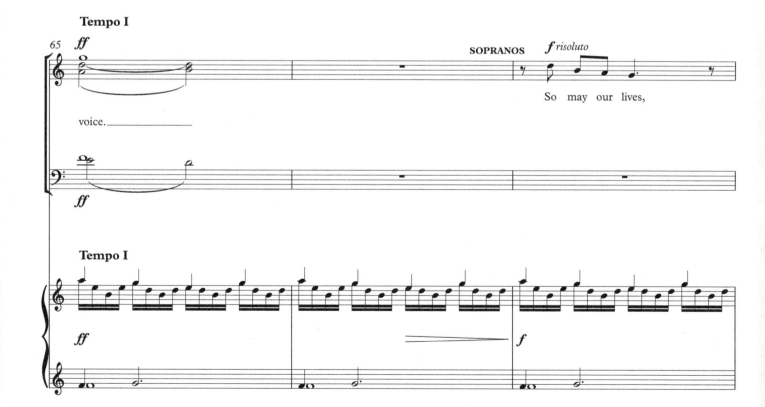

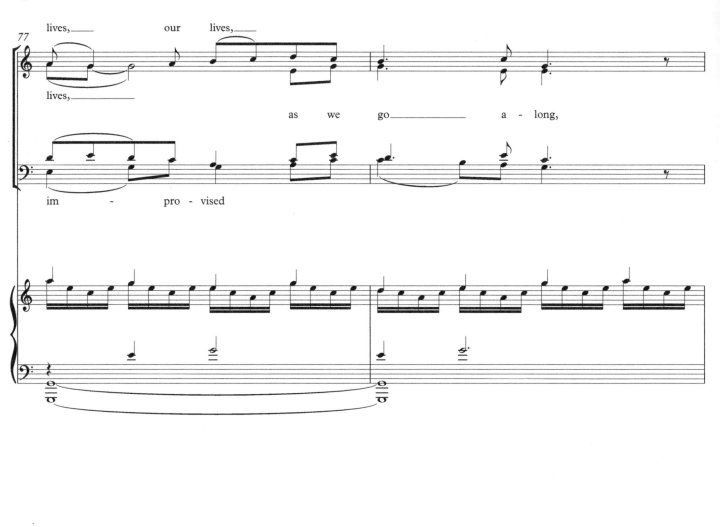

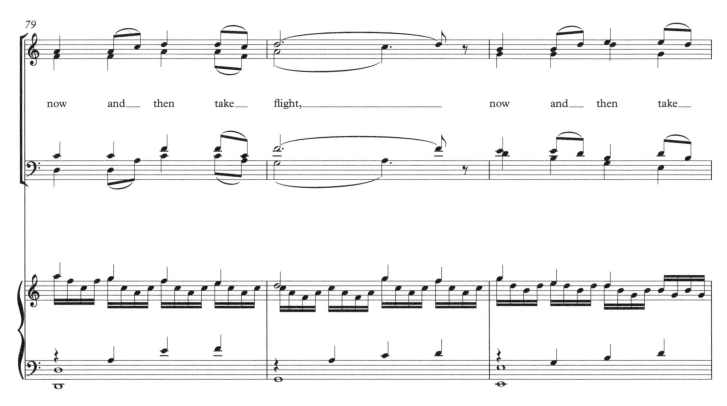

55
ah
ah
made me think: if rag - ged birds can re - joice and sing in a sea - son
58
f
I ought to spread my wings and find my
such as this,
f
f

flight,_____ now and then take flight to be - come a____

song,_____ a___ song,_____ a___ song._____